50 French Ice Cream Recipes for Home

By: Kelly Johnson

Table of Contents

- Vanilla Bean Ice Cream
- Chocolate Mousse Ice Cream
- Strawberry Sorbet
- Pistachio Gelato
- Coffee Ice Cream
- Raspberry Frozen Yogurt
- Lemon Basil Sorbet
- Hazelnut Gelato
- Mango Ice Cream
- Blackberry Sorbet
- Mint Chocolate Chip Ice Cream
- Almond Gelato
- Passion Fruit Sorbet
- Salted Caramel Ice Cream
- Coconut Sorbet
- Tiramisu Gelato
- Blood Orange Sorbet
- Cherry Almond Ice Cream
- Green Tea Gelato
- Pineapple Sorbet
- Earl Grey Ice Cream
- Lavender Honey Gelato
- Kiwi Sorbet
- White Chocolate Raspberry Ice Cream
- Pistachio Rose Gelato
- Grapefruit Sorbet
- Cardamom Ice Cream
- Caramelized Banana Gelato
- Blueberry Sorbet
- Praline Ice Cream
- Marsala Wine Gelato
- Watermelon Sorbet
- Earl Grey Lavender Ice Cream
- Nutella Gelato
- Pear Sorbet

- Salted Pistachio Ice Cream
- Lemon Thyme Gelato
- Plum Sorbet
- Spiced Apple Ice Cream
- Chocolate Hazelnut Gelato
- Fig Sorbet
- Honey Lavender Ice Cream
- Coconut Lime Gelato
- Mango Passion Fruit Sorbet
- Brown Butter Pecan Ice Cream
- Rosewater Pistachio Gelato
- Apricot Sorbet
- Bourbon Vanilla Ice Cream
- Dark Chocolate Gelato
- Champagne Sorbet

Vanilla Bean Ice Cream

Ingredients:

- 1 cup whole milk
- 2 cups heavy cream
- 3/4 cup granulated sugar
- Pinch of salt
- 1 vanilla bean pod (or 2 teaspoons vanilla extract)
- 6 large egg yolks

Instructions:

1. In a saucepan, combine the milk, heavy cream, half of the sugar, and salt. Split the vanilla bean pod lengthwise and scrape out the seeds. Add both the pod and the seeds to the saucepan. Heat the mixture over medium heat until it just begins to simmer. Remove from heat, cover, and let it steep for about 30 minutes to infuse the flavors.
2. In a separate bowl, whisk the egg yolks with the remaining sugar until pale and slightly thickened.
3. Rewarm the milk mixture over medium heat until it just starts to simmer again. Remove the vanilla bean pod.
4. Gradually pour the warm milk mixture into the egg yolks, whisking constantly to temper the eggs.
5. Pour the mixture back into the saucepan and cook over low heat, stirring constantly, until the custard thickens slightly and coats the back of a spoon (about 170-175°F or 77-80°C).
6. Strain the custard through a fine-mesh sieve into a clean bowl. Cover with plastic wrap, pressing it directly onto the surface of the custard to prevent a skin from forming. Chill in the refrigerator for at least 4 hours or overnight.
7. Once chilled, churn the custard in an ice cream maker according to the manufacturer's instructions until it reaches a soft-serve consistency.
8. Transfer the churned ice cream to a freezer-safe container, press a piece of parchment paper or plastic wrap directly onto the surface, and freeze until firm (usually 4-6 hours).
9. Serve and enjoy the creamy goodness of homemade Vanilla Bean Ice Cream!

This recipe yields about 1 quart of ice cream. Adjust sweetness or vanilla intensity to your preference by varying the amount of sugar or vanilla used.

Chocolate Mousse Ice Cream

Ingredients:

- 1 cup heavy cream
- 1/2 cup whole milk
- 1/2 cup granulated sugar
- 1/4 cup unsweetened cocoa powder
- 3 large egg yolks
- 4 ounces dark chocolate, chopped
- 1 teaspoon vanilla extract
- Pinch of salt

Instructions:

1. In a saucepan, heat the heavy cream, whole milk, sugar, and cocoa powder over medium heat, stirring constantly, until the mixture is hot and the sugar has dissolved. Do not let it boil.
2. In a separate bowl, whisk the egg yolks. Gradually pour about half of the hot cream mixture into the egg yolks, whisking constantly, to temper the yolks.
3. Pour the tempered egg mixture back into the saucepan with the remaining cream mixture. Cook over medium-low heat, stirring constantly, until the mixture thickens slightly and coats the back of a spoon (about 170-175°F or 77-80°C). Do not let it boil.
4. Remove the saucepan from heat and immediately add the chopped dark chocolate, vanilla extract, and salt. Stir until the chocolate is completely melted and the mixture is smooth.
5. Strain the mixture through a fine-mesh sieve into a clean bowl to remove any lumps or bits of egg.
6. Cover the bowl with plastic wrap, pressing it directly onto the surface of the chocolate custard to prevent a skin from forming. Chill in the refrigerator for at least 4 hours or overnight.
7. Once chilled, churn the chocolate custard in an ice cream maker according to the manufacturer's instructions until it reaches a soft-serve consistency.
8. Transfer the churned ice cream to a freezer-safe container, press a piece of parchment paper or plastic wrap directly onto the surface, and freeze until firm (usually 4-6 hours).
9. Serve and enjoy the rich and creamy Chocolate Mousse Ice Cream!

This recipe yields about 1 quart of ice cream. Adjust the cocoa powder and chocolate amount based on your preference for a darker or richer chocolate flavor.

Strawberry Sorbet

Ingredients:

- 1 pound (450g) fresh strawberries, hulled and halved
- 3/4 cup (150g) granulated sugar
- 1/4 cup (60ml) water
- 1 tablespoon fresh lemon juice

Instructions:

1. In a small saucepan, combine the sugar and water. Heat over medium heat, stirring occasionally, until the sugar has completely dissolved. Remove from heat and let the syrup cool to room temperature.
2. In a blender or food processor, puree the strawberries until smooth.
3. Pour the strawberry puree through a fine-mesh sieve into a bowl to remove the seeds (if desired).
4. Stir the cooled sugar syrup and fresh lemon juice into the strawberry puree until well combined.
5. Cover the bowl with plastic wrap, pressing it directly onto the surface of the mixture to prevent a skin from forming. Chill the mixture in the refrigerator for at least 2 hours, or until thoroughly chilled.
6. Once chilled, pour the strawberry mixture into an ice cream maker and churn according to the manufacturer's instructions until it reaches a smooth and frozen consistency.
7. Transfer the sorbet to a freezer-safe container, cover with plastic wrap or a lid, and freeze for at least 4 hours or until firm.
8. Serve the Strawberry Sorbet scooped into bowls or glasses, garnished with fresh strawberries or mint leaves if desired.

Enjoy the vibrant and refreshing taste of homemade Strawberry Sorbet! This recipe yields about 1 quart of sorbet.

Pistachio Gelato

Ingredients:

- 1 cup shelled pistachios, unsalted
- 2 cups whole milk
- 1 cup heavy cream
- 3/4 cup granulated sugar
- 1/8 teaspoon salt
- 5 large egg yolks
- 1 teaspoon vanilla extract

Instructions:

1. Preheat your oven to 350°F (175°C). Spread the pistachios evenly on a baking sheet and toast them in the oven for about 8-10 minutes, until lightly golden and fragrant. Remove from the oven and let them cool completely.
2. Once cooled, finely chop or grind the toasted pistachios in a food processor until they resemble a coarse powder.
3. In a saucepan, combine the whole milk, heavy cream, half of the sugar, salt, and ground pistachios. Heat the mixture over medium heat, stirring occasionally, until it just begins to simmer. Remove from heat, cover, and let it steep for about 30 minutes to infuse the pistachio flavor.
4. In a separate bowl, whisk together the egg yolks and the remaining sugar until pale and slightly thickened.
5. Rewarm the milk and pistachio mixture over medium heat until it just starts to simmer again. Remove from heat.
6. Gradually pour the warm milk and pistachio mixture into the egg yolks, whisking constantly to temper the eggs.
7. Pour the mixture back into the saucepan and cook over low heat, stirring constantly, until the custard thickens slightly and coats the back of a spoon (about 170-175°F or 77-80°C). Do not let it boil.
8. Strain the custard through a fine-mesh sieve into a clean bowl, pressing down on the pistachios to extract as much flavor as possible. Discard the solids.
9. Stir in the vanilla extract. Cover the bowl with plastic wrap, pressing it directly onto the surface of the custard to prevent a skin from forming. Chill in the refrigerator for at least 4 hours or overnight.
10. Once chilled, churn the pistachio custard in an ice cream maker according to the manufacturer's instructions until it reaches a soft-serve consistency.

11. Transfer the churned gelato to a freezer-safe container, press a piece of parchment paper or plastic wrap directly onto the surface, and freeze until firm (usually 4-6 hours).
12. Serve and enjoy the creamy and nutty Pistachio Gelato!

This recipe yields about 1 quart of gelato. Adjust sweetness by varying the amount of sugar used, depending on your preference.

Coffee Ice Cream

Ingredients:

- 1 1/2 cups whole milk
- 1 1/2 cups heavy cream
- 3/4 cup granulated sugar
- 1/4 teaspoon salt
- 1/4 cup instant coffee granules or espresso powder
- 6 large egg yolks
- 1 teaspoon vanilla extract

Instructions:

1. In a saucepan, combine the whole milk, heavy cream, sugar, salt, and instant coffee granules (or espresso powder). Heat over medium heat, stirring occasionally, until the mixture is hot and the sugar has completely dissolved. Do not let it boil.
2. In a separate bowl, whisk the egg yolks until smooth.
3. Gradually pour about half of the hot cream mixture into the egg yolks, whisking constantly, to temper the yolks.
4. Pour the tempered egg mixture back into the saucepan with the remaining cream mixture. Cook over medium-low heat, stirring constantly, until the mixture thickens slightly and coats the back of a spoon (about 170-175°F or 77-80°C). Do not let it boil.
5. Remove the saucepan from heat and stir in the vanilla extract.
6. Strain the mixture through a fine-mesh sieve into a clean bowl to remove any bits of egg or coffee granules.
7. Cover the bowl with plastic wrap, pressing it directly onto the surface of the custard to prevent a skin from forming. Chill in the refrigerator for at least 4 hours or overnight.
8. Once chilled, churn the coffee custard in an ice cream maker according to the manufacturer's instructions until it reaches a soft-serve consistency.
9. Transfer the churned ice cream to a freezer-safe container, press a piece of parchment paper or plastic wrap directly onto the surface, and freeze until firm (usually 4-6 hours).
10. Serve and enjoy the creamy and aromatic Coffee Ice Cream!

This recipe yields about 1 quart of ice cream. You can adjust the intensity of coffee flavor by varying the amount of instant coffee or espresso powder used.

Raspberry Frozen Yogurt

Ingredients:

- 3 cups fresh or frozen raspberries
- 1 cup plain Greek yogurt (full-fat or low-fat)
- 1/2 cup granulated sugar (adjust based on sweetness of raspberries)
- 1 tablespoon fresh lemon juice
- 1 teaspoon vanilla extract

Instructions:

1. If using frozen raspberries, thaw them slightly. If using fresh raspberries, rinse them and pat dry.
2. In a blender or food processor, puree the raspberries until smooth.
3. Pour the raspberry puree through a fine-mesh sieve into a bowl to remove the seeds (if desired).
4. In a separate bowl, whisk together the Greek yogurt, sugar, lemon juice, and vanilla extract until the sugar is dissolved and the mixture is smooth.
5. Combine the raspberry puree with the yogurt mixture, stirring until well combined.
6. Cover the bowl with plastic wrap, pressing it directly onto the surface of the mixture to prevent a skin from forming. Chill the mixture in the refrigerator for at least 2 hours, or until thoroughly chilled.
7. Once chilled, pour the raspberry yogurt mixture into an ice cream maker and churn according to the manufacturer's instructions until it reaches a smooth and frozen consistency.
8. Transfer the frozen yogurt to a freezer-safe container, cover with plastic wrap or a lid, and freeze for at least 4 hours or until firm.
9. Serve the Raspberry Frozen Yogurt scooped into bowls or cones, garnished with fresh raspberries if desired.

Enjoy the tangy and fruity goodness of homemade Raspberry Frozen Yogurt! This recipe makes about 1 quart of frozen yogurt. Adjust sweetness by varying the amount of sugar used, depending on your preference and the sweetness of the raspberries.

Lemon Basil Sorbet

Ingredients:

- 1 cup water
- 1 cup granulated sugar
- Zest of 2 lemons
- 1 cup freshly squeezed lemon juice (about 4-6 lemons)
- 1/4 cup fresh basil leaves, chopped

Instructions:

1. In a saucepan, combine the water, granulated sugar, and lemon zest. Heat over medium heat, stirring occasionally, until the sugar is completely dissolved. Remove from heat and let the syrup cool to room temperature.
2. Once cooled, strain the syrup through a fine-mesh sieve to remove the lemon zest.
3. In a blender or food processor, combine the cooled syrup, freshly squeezed lemon juice, and chopped basil leaves. Blend until the basil is finely chopped and well incorporated into the mixture.
4. Pour the mixture through a fine-mesh sieve into a bowl to remove the basil pieces and any pulp.
5. Cover the bowl with plastic wrap, pressing it directly onto the surface of the mixture to prevent a skin from forming. Chill the mixture in the refrigerator for at least 2 hours, or until thoroughly chilled.
6. Once chilled, pour the lemon basil mixture into an ice cream maker and churn according to the manufacturer's instructions until it reaches a smooth and frozen consistency.
7. Transfer the sorbet to a freezer-safe container, cover with plastic wrap or a lid, and freeze for at least 4 hours or until firm.
8. Serve the Lemon Basil Sorbet scooped into bowls or glasses, garnished with fresh basil leaves or a slice of lemon if desired.

Enjoy the bright and herbaceous flavors of homemade Lemon Basil Sorbet! This recipe makes about 1 quart of sorbet. Adjust sweetness by varying the amount of sugar used, depending on your preference for tartness.

Hazelnut Gelato

Ingredients:

- 1 cup whole milk
- 1 cup heavy cream
- 3/4 cup granulated sugar
- Pinch of salt
- 1 cup hazelnuts, toasted and skinned
- 4 large egg yolks
- 1 teaspoon vanilla extract

Instructions:

1. Preheat your oven to 350°F (175°C). Spread the hazelnuts evenly on a baking sheet and toast them in the oven for about 8-10 minutes, until lightly golden and fragrant. Remove from the oven and let them cool slightly.
2. Rub the toasted hazelnuts in a kitchen towel to remove the skins as much as possible. It's okay if some skin remains.
3. In a blender or food processor, grind the toasted hazelnuts into a fine meal.
4. In a saucepan, combine the whole milk, heavy cream, half of the sugar, and salt. Heat over medium heat, stirring occasionally, until the mixture is hot and the sugar has dissolved. Do not let it boil.
5. In a separate bowl, whisk the egg yolks with the remaining sugar until pale and slightly thickened.
6. Gradually pour about half of the hot milk mixture into the egg yolks, whisking constantly, to temper the yolks.
7. Pour the tempered egg mixture back into the saucepan with the remaining milk mixture. Cook over medium-low heat, stirring constantly, until the custard thickens slightly and coats the back of a spoon (about 170-175°F or 77-80°C). Do not let it boil.
8. Remove the saucepan from heat and immediately stir in the ground hazelnuts and vanilla extract.
9. Strain the custard through a fine-mesh sieve into a clean bowl to remove any hazelnut pieces and ensure a smooth texture.
10. Cover the bowl with plastic wrap, pressing it directly onto the surface of the custard to prevent a skin from forming. Chill in the refrigerator for at least 4 hours or overnight.
11. Once chilled, churn the hazelnut custard in an ice cream maker according to the manufacturer's instructions until it reaches a soft-serve consistency.

12. Transfer the churned gelato to a freezer-safe container, press a piece of parchment paper or plastic wrap directly onto the surface, and freeze until firm (usually 4-6 hours).
13. Serve and enjoy the creamy and nutty Hazelnut Gelato!

This recipe yields about 1 quart of gelato. Adjust sweetness by varying the amount of sugar used, depending on your preference for sweetness.

Mango Ice Cream

Ingredients:

- 2 cups ripe mango puree (from about 2-3 large mangoes)
- 1 cup whole milk
- 1 cup heavy cream
- 3/4 cup granulated sugar
- Pinch of salt
- 4 large egg yolks
- 1 teaspoon vanilla extract

Instructions:

1. Peel and chop the mangoes, then puree them in a blender or food processor until smooth. Measure out 2 cups of mango puree and set aside.
2. In a saucepan, combine the whole milk, heavy cream, half of the sugar, and salt. Heat over medium heat, stirring occasionally, until the mixture is hot and the sugar has dissolved. Do not let it boil.
3. In a separate bowl, whisk the egg yolks with the remaining sugar until pale and slightly thickened.
4. Gradually pour about half of the hot milk mixture into the egg yolks, whisking constantly, to temper the yolks.
5. Pour the tempered egg mixture back into the saucepan with the remaining milk mixture. Cook over medium-low heat, stirring constantly, until the custard thickens slightly and coats the back of a spoon (about 170-175°F or 77-80°C). Do not let it boil.
6. Remove the saucepan from heat and stir in the mango puree and vanilla extract.
7. Strain the custard through a fine-mesh sieve into a clean bowl to remove any bits of egg or mango fibers. This step helps ensure a smooth texture.
8. Cover the bowl with plastic wrap, pressing it directly onto the surface of the custard to prevent a skin from forming. Chill in the refrigerator for at least 4 hours or overnight.
9. Once chilled, churn the mango custard in an ice cream maker according to the manufacturer's instructions until it reaches a soft-serve consistency.
10. Transfer the churned mango ice cream to a freezer-safe container, press a piece of parchment paper or plastic wrap directly onto the surface, and freeze until firm (usually 4-6 hours).
11. Serve and enjoy the creamy and fruity Mango Ice Cream!

This recipe yields about 1 quart of ice cream. Adjust sweetness by varying the amount of sugar used, depending on the sweetness of the mangoes.

Blackberry Sorbet

Ingredients:

- 4 cups fresh blackberries
- 1 cup water
- 1 cup granulated sugar
- 1 tablespoon fresh lemon juice

Instructions:

1. In a small saucepan, combine the water and granulated sugar. Heat over medium heat, stirring occasionally, until the sugar is completely dissolved. Remove from heat and let the syrup cool to room temperature.
2. Rinse the blackberries thoroughly under cold water and drain.
3. In a blender or food processor, puree the blackberries until smooth.
4. Pour the blackberry puree through a fine-mesh sieve into a bowl to remove the seeds (if desired).
5. Stir the cooled sugar syrup and fresh lemon juice into the blackberry puree until well combined.
6. Cover the bowl with plastic wrap, pressing it directly onto the surface of the mixture to prevent a skin from forming. Chill the mixture in the refrigerator for at least 2 hours, or until thoroughly chilled.
7. Once chilled, pour the blackberry mixture into an ice cream maker and churn according to the manufacturer's instructions until it reaches a smooth and frozen consistency.
8. Transfer the sorbet to a freezer-safe container, cover with plastic wrap or a lid, and freeze for at least 4 hours or until firm.
9. Serve the Blackberry Sorbet scooped into bowls or cones, garnished with fresh blackberries or mint leaves if desired.

Enjoy the vibrant and fruity flavor of homemade Blackberry Sorbet! This recipe makes about 1 quart of sorbet. Adjust sweetness by varying the amount of sugar used, depending on the sweetness of the blackberries.

Mint Chocolate Chip Ice Cream

Ingredients:

- 2 cups heavy cream
- 1 cup whole milk
- 3/4 cup granulated sugar
- Pinch of salt
- 2 teaspoons pure peppermint extract
- Green food coloring (optional)
- 1 cup dark chocolate, chopped into small chunks or chips

Instructions:

1. In a saucepan, combine the heavy cream, whole milk, sugar, and salt. Heat over medium heat, stirring occasionally, until the mixture is hot and the sugar has dissolved. Do not let it boil.
2. Remove the saucepan from heat and stir in the peppermint extract. Add green food coloring if desired, to achieve a mint green color.
3. Transfer the mixture to a bowl and cover with plastic wrap, pressing it directly onto the surface of the mixture to prevent a skin from forming. Chill in the refrigerator for at least 4 hours or overnight.
4. Once chilled, churn the mint ice cream base in an ice cream maker according to the manufacturer's instructions until it reaches a soft-serve consistency.
5. During the last few minutes of churning, add the chopped dark chocolate and let it mix evenly into the ice cream.
6. Transfer the churned ice cream to a freezer-safe container, press a piece of parchment paper or plastic wrap directly onto the surface, and freeze until firm (usually 4-6 hours).
7. Serve and enjoy the refreshing and creamy Mint Chocolate Chip Ice Cream!

This recipe yields about 1 quart of ice cream. Adjust the amount of peppermint extract to your taste preference. You can also vary the intensity of chocolate chips according to your liking.

Almond Gelato

Ingredients:

- 1 cup whole milk
- 1 cup heavy cream
- 3/4 cup granulated sugar
- Pinch of salt
- 1 cup almond milk (unsweetened)
- 1/2 cup almond paste or almond butter
- 4 large egg yolks
- 1 teaspoon almond extract
- 1/2 cup sliced almonds, toasted (optional, for garnish)

Instructions:

1. In a saucepan, combine the whole milk, heavy cream, sugar, and salt. Heat over medium heat, stirring occasionally, until the mixture is hot and the sugar has dissolved. Do not let it boil.
2. In a separate bowl, whisk the egg yolks until smooth.
3. Gradually pour about half of the hot milk mixture into the egg yolks, whisking constantly, to temper the yolks.
4. Pour the tempered egg mixture back into the saucepan with the remaining milk mixture. Cook over medium-low heat, stirring constantly, until the custard thickens slightly and coats the back of a spoon (about 170-175°F or 77-80°C). Do not let it boil.
5. Remove the saucepan from heat and immediately stir in the almond milk and almond paste (or almond butter) until well combined.
6. Stir in the almond extract.
7. Strain the custard through a fine-mesh sieve into a clean bowl to ensure a smooth texture.
8. Cover the bowl with plastic wrap, pressing it directly onto the surface of the custard to prevent a skin from forming. Chill in the refrigerator for at least 4 hours or overnight.
9. Once chilled, churn the almond custard in an ice cream maker according to the manufacturer's instructions until it reaches a soft-serve consistency.
10. Transfer the churned gelato to a freezer-safe container, press a piece of parchment paper or plastic wrap directly onto the surface, and freeze until firm (usually 4-6 hours).
11. Serve the Almond Gelato garnished with toasted sliced almonds if desired.

Enjoy the creamy and nutty flavor of homemade Almond Gelato! This recipe yields about 1 quart of gelato. Adjust sweetness by varying the amount of sugar used, depending on your preference.

Passion Fruit Sorbet

Ingredients:

- 1 cup water
- 1 cup granulated sugar
- 1 cup fresh passion fruit pulp (about 6-8 passion fruits)
- 1 tablespoon fresh lemon juice

Instructions:

1. In a small saucepan, combine the water and granulated sugar. Heat over medium heat, stirring occasionally, until the sugar is completely dissolved. Remove from heat and let the syrup cool to room temperature.
2. Cut the passion fruits in half and scoop out the pulp and seeds into a bowl.
3. In a blender or food processor, puree the passion fruit pulp until smooth.
4. Pour the passion fruit puree through a fine-mesh sieve into a bowl to remove the seeds and any large pieces of pulp.
5. Stir the cooled sugar syrup and fresh lemon juice into the passion fruit puree until well combined.
6. Cover the bowl with plastic wrap, pressing it directly onto the surface of the mixture to prevent a skin from forming. Chill the mixture in the refrigerator for at least 2 hours, or until thoroughly chilled.
7. Once chilled, pour the passion fruit mixture into an ice cream maker and churn according to the manufacturer's instructions until it reaches a smooth and frozen consistency.
8. Transfer the sorbet to a freezer-safe container, cover with plastic wrap or a lid, and freeze for at least 4 hours or until firm.
9. Serve the Passion Fruit Sorbet scooped into bowls or cones, garnished with fresh mint leaves or a slice of passion fruit if desired.

Enjoy the tropical and tangy flavors of homemade Passion Fruit Sorbet! This recipe makes about 1 quart of sorbet. Adjust sweetness by varying the amount of sugar used, depending on the tartness of the passion fruits.

Salted Caramel Ice Cream

Ingredients:

- 1 cup granulated sugar
- 1/4 cup water
- 2 cups heavy cream
- 1 cup whole milk
- 1 teaspoon vanilla extract
- 6 large egg yolks
- 1/2 teaspoon sea salt (plus extra for sprinkling)

Instructions:

1. In a heavy-bottomed saucepan, combine the granulated sugar and water over medium heat. Stir until the sugar dissolves.
2. Once the sugar has dissolved, stop stirring and let the mixture come to a boil. Continue boiling, swirling the pan occasionally, until the mixture turns a deep amber color (be careful not to burn it). This should take about 5-7 minutes.
3. Immediately remove the caramel from heat and slowly whisk in the heavy cream (be cautious as it will bubble up vigorously). Stir until smooth.
4. Return the caramel mixture to low heat and stir in the whole milk and vanilla extract. Heat until the mixture is warm.
5. In a separate bowl, whisk the egg yolks until smooth. Gradually pour about half of the warm caramel mixture into the egg yolks, whisking constantly, to temper the yolks.
6. Pour the tempered egg mixture back into the saucepan with the remaining caramel mixture. Cook over medium-low heat, stirring constantly, until the custard thickens slightly and coats the back of a spoon (about 170-175°F or 77-80°C). Do not let it boil.
7. Remove the saucepan from heat and stir in the sea salt. Taste and adjust saltiness if needed.
8. Strain the custard through a fine-mesh sieve into a clean bowl to remove any bits of cooked egg or caramel lumps.
9. Cover the bowl with plastic wrap, pressing it directly onto the surface of the custard to prevent a skin from forming. Chill in the refrigerator for at least 4 hours or overnight.
10. Once chilled, churn the caramel custard in an ice cream maker according to the manufacturer's instructions until it reaches a soft-serve consistency.

11. Transfer the churned ice cream to a freezer-safe container, sprinkle with a little sea salt on top if desired, and freeze until firm (usually 4-6 hours).
12. Serve and enjoy the rich and creamy Salted Caramel Ice Cream!

This recipe yields about 1 quart of ice cream. Adjust sweetness and saltiness according to your taste preferences.

Coconut Sorbet

Ingredients:

- 2 cans (13.5 oz each) full-fat coconut milk
- 3/4 cup granulated sugar
- Pinch of salt
- 1 teaspoon vanilla extract
- 1 cup shredded coconut (optional, for texture)

Instructions:

1. In a saucepan, combine the coconut milk, granulated sugar, and salt. Heat over medium heat, stirring occasionally, until the mixture is hot and the sugar has dissolved. Do not let it boil.
2. Remove the saucepan from heat and stir in the vanilla extract.
3. If using shredded coconut for texture, stir it into the coconut milk mixture.
4. Transfer the mixture to a bowl and let it cool to room temperature.
5. Cover the bowl with plastic wrap, pressing it directly onto the surface of the mixture to prevent a skin from forming. Chill in the refrigerator for at least 2 hours, or until thoroughly chilled.
6. Once chilled, pour the coconut mixture into an ice cream maker and churn according to the manufacturer's instructions until it reaches a smooth and frozen consistency.
7. Transfer the sorbet to a freezer-safe container, cover with plastic wrap or a lid, and freeze for at least 4 hours or until firm.
8. Serve the Coconut Sorbet scooped into bowls or cones.

Enjoy the tropical and creamy flavor of homemade Coconut Sorbet! This recipe makes about 1 quart of sorbet. Adjust sweetness by varying the amount of sugar used, depending on your preference.

Tiramisu Gelato

Ingredients:

- 1 1/2 cups whole milk
- 1 1/2 cups heavy cream
- 1/2 cup granulated sugar
- 4 large egg yolks
- 1/4 cup mascarpone cheese
- 1/4 cup brewed espresso or strong coffee, cooled
- 2 tablespoons coffee liqueur (such as Kahlua) (optional)
- 1 teaspoon vanilla extract
- 1/2 cup ladyfinger cookies, chopped into small pieces
- 2 tablespoons unsweetened cocoa powder, for dusting

Instructions:

1. In a saucepan, combine the whole milk, heavy cream, and half of the sugar. Heat over medium heat, stirring occasionally, until the mixture is hot and the sugar has dissolved. Do not let it boil.
2. In a separate bowl, whisk the egg yolks with the remaining sugar until pale and slightly thickened.
3. Gradually pour about half of the hot milk mixture into the egg yolks, whisking constantly, to temper the yolks.
4. Pour the tempered egg mixture back into the saucepan with the remaining milk mixture. Cook over medium-low heat, stirring constantly, until the custard thickens slightly and coats the back of a spoon (about 170-175°F or 77-80°C). Do not let it boil.
5. Remove the saucepan from heat and whisk in the mascarpone cheese until smooth and well incorporated.
6. Stir in the brewed espresso (or coffee), coffee liqueur (if using), and vanilla extract.
7. Strain the custard through a fine-mesh sieve into a clean bowl to ensure a smooth texture.
8. Cover the bowl with plastic wrap, pressing it directly onto the surface of the custard to prevent a skin from forming. Chill in the refrigerator for at least 4 hours or overnight.
9. Once chilled, churn the tiramisu custard in an ice cream maker according to the manufacturer's instructions until it reaches a soft-serve consistency.

10. During the last few minutes of churning, add the chopped ladyfinger cookies and let them mix evenly into the gelato.
11. Transfer the churned tiramisu gelato to a freezer-safe container, sprinkle the top with unsweetened cocoa powder, and freeze until firm (usually 4-6 hours).
12. Serve the Tiramisu Gelato scooped into bowls or cones, dusted with additional cocoa powder if desired.

Enjoy the rich flavors of Tiramisu in a creamy and frozen form with this delicious homemade gelato! Adjust sweetness and intensity of coffee flavors to your preference.

Blood Orange Sorbet

Ingredients:

- 2 cups fresh blood orange juice (from about 6-8 blood oranges)
- 1 cup water
- 1 cup granulated sugar
- Zest of 1 blood orange (optional, for extra flavor)

Instructions:

1. In a small saucepan, combine the water and granulated sugar. Heat over medium heat, stirring occasionally, until the sugar is completely dissolved. Remove from heat and let the syrup cool to room temperature.
2. While the syrup is cooling, juice the blood oranges to get 2 cups of juice. If using, zest one of the blood oranges and set aside.
3. In a blender or food processor, combine the blood orange juice and cooled sugar syrup. Blend until well combined.
4. If using, stir in the blood orange zest for added flavor.
5. Pour the mixture through a fine-mesh sieve into a bowl to remove any pulp or seeds.
6. Cover the bowl with plastic wrap, pressing it directly onto the surface of the mixture to prevent a skin from forming. Chill the mixture in the refrigerator for at least 2 hours, or until thoroughly chilled.
7. Once chilled, pour the blood orange mixture into an ice cream maker and churn according to the manufacturer's instructions until it reaches a smooth and frozen consistency.
8. Transfer the sorbet to a freezer-safe container, cover with plastic wrap or a lid, and freeze for at least 4 hours or until firm.
9. Serve the Blood Orange Sorbet scooped into bowls or cones, garnished with a slice of blood orange or fresh mint leaves if desired.

Enjoy the vibrant and citrusy flavors of homemade Blood Orange Sorbet! This recipe makes about 1 quart of sorbet. Adjust sweetness by varying the amount of sugar used, depending on the tartness of the blood oranges.

Cherry Almond Ice Cream

Ingredients:

- 2 cups pitted cherries, fresh or frozen
- 1 cup whole milk
- 1 cup heavy cream
- 3/4 cup granulated sugar
- Pinch of salt
- 4 large egg yolks
- 1 teaspoon almond extract
- 1/2 cup sliced almonds, toasted (optional, for garnish)

Instructions:

1. In a blender or food processor, puree the pitted cherries until smooth. Set aside.
2. In a saucepan, combine the whole milk, heavy cream, half of the sugar, and salt. Heat over medium heat, stirring occasionally, until the mixture is hot and the sugar has dissolved. Do not let it boil.
3. In a separate bowl, whisk the egg yolks with the remaining sugar until pale and slightly thickened.
4. Gradually pour about half of the hot milk mixture into the egg yolks, whisking constantly, to temper the yolks.
5. Pour the tempered egg mixture back into the saucepan with the remaining milk mixture. Cook over medium-low heat, stirring constantly, until the custard thickens slightly and coats the back of a spoon (about 170-175°F or 77-80°C). Do not let it boil.
6. Remove the saucepan from heat and stir in the cherry puree and almond extract until well combined.
7. Strain the custard through a fine-mesh sieve into a clean bowl to remove any bits of cooked egg or cherry fibers.
8. Cover the bowl with plastic wrap, pressing it directly onto the surface of the custard to prevent a skin from forming. Chill in the refrigerator for at least 4 hours or overnight.
9. Once chilled, churn the cherry custard in an ice cream maker according to the manufacturer's instructions until it reaches a soft-serve consistency.
10. During the last few minutes of churning, add the toasted sliced almonds if using, and let them mix evenly into the ice cream.

11. Transfer the churned ice cream to a freezer-safe container, press a piece of parchment paper or plastic wrap directly onto the surface, and freeze until firm (usually 4-6 hours).
12. Serve the Cherry Almond Ice Cream scooped into bowls or cones, garnished with additional toasted almonds if desired.

Enjoy the creamy and fruity flavors of homemade Cherry Almond Ice Cream! This recipe yields about 1 quart of ice cream. Adjust sweetness by varying the amount of sugar used, depending on the sweetness of the cherries.

Green Tea Gelato

Ingredients:

- 2 cups whole milk
- 1 cup heavy cream
- 3/4 cup granulated sugar
- 3 tablespoons matcha green tea powder
- Pinch of salt
- 4 large egg yolks
- 1 teaspoon vanilla extract

Instructions:

1. In a saucepan, combine the whole milk, heavy cream, half of the sugar, matcha green tea powder, and salt. Whisk together until the matcha powder is fully dissolved.
2. Heat the mixture over medium heat, stirring occasionally, until it is hot and just begins to bubble around the edges. Do not let it boil.
3. In a separate bowl, whisk the egg yolks with the remaining sugar until pale and slightly thickened.
4. Gradually pour about half of the hot milk mixture into the egg yolks, whisking constantly, to temper the yolks.
5. Pour the tempered egg mixture back into the saucepan with the remaining milk mixture. Cook over medium-low heat, stirring constantly, until the custard thickens slightly and coats the back of a spoon (about 170-175°F or 77-80°C). Do not let it boil.
6. Remove the saucepan from heat and stir in the vanilla extract.
7. Strain the custard through a fine-mesh sieve into a clean bowl to remove any bits of cooked egg or undissolved matcha powder.
8. Cover the bowl with plastic wrap, pressing it directly onto the surface of the custard to prevent a skin from forming. Chill in the refrigerator for at least 4 hours or overnight.
9. Once chilled, churn the green tea custard in an ice cream maker according to the manufacturer's instructions until it reaches a soft-serve consistency.
10. Transfer the churned gelato to a freezer-safe container, press a piece of parchment paper or plastic wrap directly onto the surface, and freeze until firm (usually 4-6 hours).
11. Serve the Green Tea Gelato scooped into bowls or cones.

Enjoy the creamy and slightly bitter-sweet flavors of homemade Green Tea Gelato! This recipe makes about 1 quart of gelato. Adjust sweetness by varying the amount of sugar used, depending on your preference for sweetness and the quality of matcha powder used.

Pineapple Sorbet

Ingredients:

- 1 ripe pineapple, peeled, cored, and chopped (about 4 cups)
- 1 cup water
- 3/4 cup granulated sugar
- Juice of 1 lime (optional, for added brightness)

Instructions:

1. In a small saucepan, combine the water and granulated sugar. Heat over medium heat, stirring occasionally, until the sugar is completely dissolved. Remove from heat and let the syrup cool to room temperature.
2. In a blender or food processor, puree the chopped pineapple until smooth.
3. Pour the pineapple puree through a fine-mesh sieve into a bowl to remove any fibrous pieces.
4. Stir in the cooled sugar syrup and lime juice (if using) into the pineapple puree until well combined.
5. Cover the bowl with plastic wrap, pressing it directly onto the surface of the mixture to prevent a skin from forming. Chill the mixture in the refrigerator for at least 2 hours, or until thoroughly chilled.
6. Once chilled, pour the pineapple mixture into an ice cream maker and churn according to the manufacturer's instructions until it reaches a smooth and frozen consistency.
7. Transfer the sorbet to a freezer-safe container, cover with plastic wrap or a lid, and freeze for at least 4 hours or until firm.
8. Serve the Pineapple Sorbet scooped into bowls or cones, garnished with a pineapple slice or mint leaves if desired.

Enjoy the tropical and fruity flavors of homemade Pineapple Sorbet! This recipe makes about 1 quart of sorbet. Adjust sweetness by varying the amount of sugar used, depending on the sweetness of the pineapple.

Earl Grey Ice Cream

Ingredients:

- 2 cups heavy cream
- 1 cup whole milk
- 3/4 cup granulated sugar
- Pinch of salt
- 3 tablespoons loose Earl Grey tea leaves (or 4-5 Earl Grey tea bags)
- 5 large egg yolks
- 1 teaspoon vanilla extract

Instructions:

1. In a saucepan, combine the heavy cream, whole milk, half of the sugar, salt, and Earl Grey tea leaves (or tea bags). Heat over medium heat, stirring occasionally, until the mixture is hot and just begins to bubble around the edges. Do not let it boil.
2. Remove the saucepan from heat, cover, and let the Earl Grey tea steep in the cream mixture for about 15-20 minutes to infuse the flavors. Stir occasionally.
3. Strain the infused cream mixture through a fine-mesh sieve into a clean saucepan, pressing on the tea leaves to extract all the liquid. Discard the tea leaves (or tea bags).
4. In a separate bowl, whisk the egg yolks with the remaining sugar until pale and slightly thickened.
5. Gradually pour about half of the hot infused cream mixture into the egg yolks, whisking constantly, to temper the yolks.
6. Pour the tempered egg mixture back into the saucepan with the remaining infused cream mixture. Cook over medium-low heat, stirring constantly, until the custard thickens slightly and coats the back of a spoon (about 170-175°F or 77-80°C). Do not let it boil.
7. Remove the saucepan from heat and stir in the vanilla extract.
8. Strain the custard through a fine-mesh sieve into a clean bowl to remove any bits of cooked egg or tea leaves.
9. Cover the bowl with plastic wrap, pressing it directly onto the surface of the custard to prevent a skin from forming. Chill in the refrigerator for at least 4 hours or overnight.
10. Once chilled, churn the Earl Grey custard in an ice cream maker according to the manufacturer's instructions until it reaches a soft-serve consistency.

11. Transfer the churned ice cream to a freezer-safe container, press a piece of parchment paper or plastic wrap directly onto the surface, and freeze until firm (usually 4-6 hours).
12. Serve the Earl Grey Ice Cream scooped into bowls or cones.

Enjoy the elegant and aromatic flavors of homemade Earl Grey Ice Cream! This recipe yields about 1 quart of ice cream. Adjust sweetness and intensity of tea flavor by varying the amount of sugar and tea leaves used, according to your preference.

Lavender Honey Gelato

Ingredients:

- 2 cups whole milk
- 1 cup heavy cream
- 1/2 cup granulated sugar
- 2 tablespoons dried culinary lavender buds
- Pinch of salt
- 1/2 cup honey
- 4 large egg yolks
- 1 teaspoon vanilla extract

Instructions:

1. In a saucepan, combine the whole milk, heavy cream, half of the sugar, dried lavender buds, and salt. Heat over medium heat, stirring occasionally, until the mixture is hot and just begins to bubble around the edges. Do not let it boil.
2. Remove the saucepan from heat, cover, and let the lavender steep in the cream mixture for about 15-20 minutes to infuse the flavors. Stir occasionally.
3. Strain the infused cream mixture through a fine-mesh sieve into a clean saucepan, pressing on the lavender buds to extract all the liquid. Discard the lavender buds.
4. In a separate bowl, whisk the egg yolks with the remaining sugar until pale and slightly thickened.
5. Gradually pour about half of the hot infused cream mixture into the egg yolks, whisking constantly, to temper the yolks.
6. Pour the tempered egg mixture back into the saucepan with the remaining infused cream mixture. Cook over medium-low heat, stirring constantly, until the custard thickens slightly and coats the back of a spoon (about 170-175°F or 77-80°C). Do not let it boil.
7. Remove the saucepan from heat and stir in the honey and vanilla extract until well combined.
8. Strain the custard through a fine-mesh sieve into a clean bowl to remove any bits of cooked egg or lavender remnants.
9. Cover the bowl with plastic wrap, pressing it directly onto the surface of the custard to prevent a skin from forming. Chill in the refrigerator for at least 4 hours or overnight.
10. Once chilled, churn the lavender honey custard in an ice cream maker according to the manufacturer's instructions until it reaches a soft-serve consistency.

11. Transfer the churned gelato to a freezer-safe container, press a piece of parchment paper or plastic wrap directly onto the surface, and freeze until firm (usually 4-6 hours).
12. Serve the Lavender Honey Gelato scooped into bowls or cones.

Enjoy the delicate floral and honey flavors of homemade Lavender Honey Gelato! This recipe yields about 1 quart of gelato. Adjust sweetness and intensity of lavender flavor by varying the amount of honey and lavender buds used, according to your preference.

Kiwi Sorbet

Ingredients:

- 6 ripe kiwi fruits, peeled and roughly chopped
- 1/2 cup water
- 1/2 cup granulated sugar
- Juice of 1 lemon or lime

Instructions:

1. In a small saucepan, combine the water and granulated sugar. Heat over medium heat, stirring occasionally, until the sugar is completely dissolved. Remove from heat and let the syrup cool to room temperature.
2. In a blender or food processor, puree the chopped kiwi fruits until smooth.
3. Pour the kiwi puree through a fine-mesh sieve into a bowl to remove any seeds or fibers.
4. Stir in the cooled sugar syrup and lemon or lime juice into the kiwi puree until well combined.
5. Cover the bowl with plastic wrap, pressing it directly onto the surface of the mixture to prevent a skin from forming. Chill the mixture in the refrigerator for at least 2 hours, or until thoroughly chilled.
6. Once chilled, pour the kiwi mixture into an ice cream maker and churn according to the manufacturer's instructions until it reaches a smooth and frozen consistency.
7. Transfer the sorbet to a freezer-safe container, cover with plastic wrap or a lid, and freeze for at least 4 hours or until firm.
8. Serve the Kiwi Sorbet scooped into bowls or cones, garnished with a slice of kiwi fruit or mint leaves if desired.

Enjoy the tangy and fruity flavors of homemade Kiwi Sorbet! This recipe makes about 1 quart of sorbet. Adjust sweetness by varying the amount of sugar used, depending on the sweetness of the kiwi fruits.

White Chocolate Raspberry Ice Cream

Ingredients:

- 1 cup fresh or frozen raspberries
- 2 tablespoons granulated sugar
- 8 ounces white chocolate, chopped
- 2 cups heavy cream
- 1 cup whole milk
- 1/2 cup granulated sugar
- 4 large egg yolks
- 1 teaspoon vanilla extract

Instructions:

1. In a small saucepan, combine the raspberries and 2 tablespoons of sugar. Cook over medium heat, stirring occasionally, until the raspberries break down and release their juices. Simmer for about 5-7 minutes, then remove from heat and let it cool slightly. Once cooled, puree the raspberries in a blender or food processor until smooth. Strain through a fine-mesh sieve to remove seeds, if desired. Set aside.
2. In another saucepan, heat the heavy cream and whole milk over medium heat until it just begins to simmer. Remove from heat and add the chopped white chocolate. Stir until the chocolate is completely melted and smooth. Set aside.
3. In a bowl, whisk together the egg yolks and remaining 1/2 cup of granulated sugar until pale and slightly thickened.
4. Gradually pour the warm white chocolate cream mixture into the egg yolks, whisking constantly to temper the eggs.
5. Return the mixture to the saucepan and cook over medium-low heat, stirring constantly, until it thickens slightly and coats the back of a spoon (about 170-175°F or 77-80°C). Do not let it boil.
6. Remove from heat and stir in the vanilla extract. Allow the custard to cool slightly.
7. Stir the raspberry puree into the custard mixture until well combined.
8. Cover the bowl with plastic wrap, pressing it directly onto the surface of the custard to prevent a skin from forming. Chill in the refrigerator for at least 4 hours or overnight.
9. Once chilled, churn the custard mixture in an ice cream maker according to the manufacturer's instructions until it reaches a soft-serve consistency.
10. Transfer the churned ice cream to a freezer-safe container, cover with plastic wrap or a lid, and freeze until firm (usually 4-6 hours).

11. Serve the White Chocolate Raspberry Ice Cream scooped into bowls or cones, garnished with fresh raspberries or white chocolate curls if desired.

Enjoy the creamy and fruity flavors of homemade White Chocolate Raspberry Ice Cream! This recipe yields about 1 quart of ice cream. Adjust sweetness by varying the amount of sugar used, depending on the tartness of the raspberries and your preference for sweetness.

Pistachio Rose Gelato

Ingredients:

- 1 cup shelled pistachios, unsalted
- 2 cups whole milk
- 1 cup heavy cream
- 3/4 cup granulated sugar
- Pinch of salt
- 4 large egg yolks
- 1 teaspoon rose water
- 1/2 teaspoon vanilla extract
- Pink food coloring (optional, for a subtle pink hue)

Instructions:

1. Preheat your oven to 350°F (175°C). Spread the pistachios on a baking sheet in a single layer and toast them in the oven for about 8-10 minutes, or until fragrant and lightly golden. Remove from the oven and let them cool completely.
2. Once cooled, finely chop the toasted pistachios or pulse them in a food processor until coarsely ground. Set aside.
3. In a saucepan, combine the whole milk, heavy cream, half of the sugar, and salt. Heat over medium heat, stirring occasionally, until the mixture is hot and just begins to bubble around the edges. Do not let it boil.
4. Remove the saucepan from heat and stir in the ground pistachios. Cover and let the mixture steep for about 30 minutes to infuse the pistachio flavor.
5. After steeping, strain the pistachio-infused cream mixture through a fine-mesh sieve into a clean saucepan, pressing on the pistachios to extract all the liquid. Discard the pistachio solids.
6. In a separate bowl, whisk the egg yolks with the remaining sugar until pale and slightly thickened.
7. Gradually pour about half of the hot pistachio-infused cream mixture into the egg yolks, whisking constantly, to temper the yolks.
8. Pour the tempered egg mixture back into the saucepan with the remaining infused cream mixture. Cook over medium-low heat, stirring constantly, until the custard thickens slightly and coats the back of a spoon (about 170-175°F or 77-80°C). Do not let it boil.
9. Remove the saucepan from heat and stir in the rose water and vanilla extract. Add a few drops of pink food coloring if desired, stirring until evenly distributed.

10. Strain the custard through a fine-mesh sieve into a clean bowl to remove any bits of cooked egg or pistachio particles.
11. Cover the bowl with plastic wrap, pressing it directly onto the surface of the custard to prevent a skin from forming. Chill in the refrigerator for at least 4 hours or overnight.
12. Once chilled, churn the pistachio rose custard in an ice cream maker according to the manufacturer's instructions until it reaches a soft-serve consistency.
13. Transfer the churned gelato to a freezer-safe container, press a piece of parchment paper or plastic wrap directly onto the surface, and freeze until firm (usually 4-6 hours).
14. Serve the Pistachio Rose Gelato scooped into bowls or cones, garnished with chopped pistachios or edible rose petals if desired.

Enjoy the delicate and aromatic flavors of homemade Pistachio Rose Gelato! This recipe makes about 1 quart of gelato. Adjust sweetness and intensity of rose flavor by varying the amount of rose water used, according to your preference.

Grapefruit Sorbet

Ingredients:

- 2 cups fresh grapefruit juice (from about 3-4 grapefruits)
- 1 cup water
- 3/4 cup granulated sugar
- Zest of 1 grapefruit (optional, for extra flavor)

Instructions:

1. In a small saucepan, combine the water and granulated sugar. Heat over medium heat, stirring occasionally, until the sugar is completely dissolved. Remove from heat and let the syrup cool to room temperature.
2. While the syrup is cooling, juice the grapefruits to get 2 cups of grapefruit juice. If using, zest one of the grapefruits and set aside.
3. In a blender or food processor, combine the grapefruit juice and cooled sugar syrup. Blend until well combined.
4. If using, stir in the grapefruit zest for added flavor.
5. Pour the mixture through a fine-mesh sieve into a bowl to remove any pulp or seeds.
6. Cover the bowl with plastic wrap, pressing it directly onto the surface of the mixture to prevent a skin from forming. Chill the mixture in the refrigerator for at least 2 hours, or until thoroughly chilled.
7. Once chilled, pour the grapefruit mixture into an ice cream maker and churn according to the manufacturer's instructions until it reaches a smooth and frozen consistency.
8. Transfer the sorbet to a freezer-safe container, cover with plastic wrap or a lid, and freeze for at least 4 hours or until firm.
9. Serve the Grapefruit Sorbet scooped into bowls or cones, garnished with a slice of grapefruit or mint leaves if desired.

Enjoy the tangy and citrusy flavors of homemade Grapefruit Sorbet! This recipe makes about 1 quart of sorbet. Adjust sweetness by varying the amount of sugar used, depending on the tartness of the grapefruits.

Cardamom Ice Cream

Ingredients:

- 2 cups heavy cream
- 1 cup whole milk
- 3/4 cup granulated sugar
- Pinch of salt
- 10-12 cardamom pods, lightly crushed (or 1-2 teaspoons ground cardamom)
- 4 large egg yolks
- 1 teaspoon vanilla extract

Instructions:

1. In a saucepan, combine the heavy cream, whole milk, half of the sugar, salt, and crushed cardamom pods (if using whole pods). Heat over medium heat, stirring occasionally, until the mixture is hot and just begins to bubble around the edges. Do not let it boil.
2. Remove the saucepan from heat, cover, and let the cardamom steep in the cream mixture for about 15-20 minutes to infuse the flavors. Stir occasionally. If using ground cardamom, skip this steeping process.
3. Strain the infused cream mixture through a fine-mesh sieve into a clean saucepan, pressing on the cardamom pods to extract all the liquid. Discard the cardamom pods (if using whole pods).
4. In a separate bowl, whisk the egg yolks with the remaining sugar until pale and slightly thickened.
5. Gradually pour about half of the hot infused cream mixture into the egg yolks, whisking constantly, to temper the yolks.
6. Pour the tempered egg mixture back into the saucepan with the remaining infused cream mixture. Cook over medium-low heat, stirring constantly, until the custard thickens slightly and coats the back of a spoon (about 170-175°F or 77-80°C). Do not let it boil.
7. Remove the saucepan from heat and stir in the vanilla extract.
8. Strain the custard through a fine-mesh sieve into a clean bowl to remove any bits of cooked egg or cardamom remnants.
9. Cover the bowl with plastic wrap, pressing it directly onto the surface of the custard to prevent a skin from forming. Chill in the refrigerator for at least 4 hours or overnight.
10. Once chilled, churn the cardamom custard in an ice cream maker according to the manufacturer's instructions until it reaches a soft-serve consistency.

11. Transfer the churned ice cream to a freezer-safe container, press a piece of parchment paper or plastic wrap directly onto the surface, and freeze until firm (usually 4-6 hours).
12. Serve the Cardamom Ice Cream scooped into bowls or cones.

Enjoy the aromatic and exotic flavors of homemade Cardamom Ice Cream! This recipe yields about 1 quart of ice cream. Adjust the amount of cardamom used based on your preference for its intensity.

Caramelized Banana Gelato

Ingredients:

- 4 ripe bananas
- 1/2 cup granulated sugar
- 2 tablespoons unsalted butter
- 2 cups whole milk
- 1 cup heavy cream
- 3/4 cup granulated sugar
- Pinch of salt
- 4 large egg yolks
- 1 teaspoon vanilla extract

Instructions:

1. Start by preparing the caramelized bananas: Peel the bananas and slice them into 1/2-inch thick rounds.
2. In a large skillet, melt the butter over medium heat. Add the sugar and cook, stirring constantly, until the sugar melts and starts to caramelize.
3. Carefully add the banana slices to the caramelized sugar, stirring gently to coat them evenly. Cook for about 2-3 minutes on each side, until the bananas are caramelized and softened. Remove from heat and let them cool slightly.
4. In a saucepan, combine the whole milk, heavy cream, half of the sugar, and pinch of salt. Heat over medium heat, stirring occasionally, until the mixture is hot and just begins to bubble around the edges. Do not let it boil.
5. In a separate bowl, whisk the egg yolks with the remaining sugar until pale and slightly thickened.
6. Gradually pour about half of the hot milk mixture into the egg yolks, whisking constantly, to temper the yolks.
7. Pour the tempered egg mixture back into the saucepan with the remaining milk mixture. Cook over medium-low heat, stirring constantly, until the custard thickens slightly and coats the back of a spoon (about 170-175°F or 77-80°C). Do not let it boil.
8. Remove the saucepan from heat and stir in the vanilla extract.
9. In a blender or food processor, puree the caramelized banana slices until smooth.
10. Strain the banana puree through a fine-mesh sieve into the custard mixture to remove any fibrous bits or banana solids. Stir well to combine.

11. Cover the bowl with plastic wrap, pressing it directly onto the surface of the custard to prevent a skin from forming. Chill in the refrigerator for at least 4 hours or overnight.
12. Once chilled, churn the banana custard in an ice cream maker according to the manufacturer's instructions until it reaches a soft-serve consistency.
13. Transfer the churned gelato to a freezer-safe container, press a piece of parchment paper or plastic wrap directly onto the surface, and freeze until firm (usually 4-6 hours).
14. Serve the Caramelized Banana Gelato scooped into bowls or cones.

Enjoy the rich and caramelized flavors of homemade Caramelized Banana Gelato! This recipe makes about 1 quart of gelato. Adjust sweetness by varying the amount of sugar used, depending on the ripeness of the bananas and your preference for sweetness.

Blueberry Sorbet

Ingredients:

- 4 cups fresh or frozen blueberries
- 1 cup water
- 3/4 cup granulated sugar
- Juice of 1 lemon

Instructions:

1. In a small saucepan, combine the water and granulated sugar. Heat over medium heat, stirring occasionally, until the sugar is completely dissolved. Remove from heat and let the syrup cool to room temperature.
2. In a blender or food processor, puree the blueberries until smooth.
3. Pour the blueberry puree through a fine-mesh sieve into a bowl to remove any skins or seeds.
4. Stir in the cooled sugar syrup and lemon juice into the blueberry puree until well combined.
5. Cover the bowl with plastic wrap, pressing it directly onto the surface of the mixture to prevent a skin from forming. Chill the mixture in the refrigerator for at least 2 hours, or until thoroughly chilled.
6. Once chilled, pour the blueberry mixture into an ice cream maker and churn according to the manufacturer's instructions until it reaches a smooth and frozen consistency.
7. Transfer the sorbet to a freezer-safe container, cover with plastic wrap or a lid, and freeze for at least 4 hours or until firm.
8. Serve the Blueberry Sorbet scooped into bowls or cones, garnished with fresh blueberries or mint leaves if desired.

Enjoy the tangy and fruity flavors of homemade Blueberry Sorbet! This recipe makes about 1 quart of sorbet. Adjust sweetness by varying the amount of sugar used, depending on the tartness of the blueberries and your preference.

Praline Ice Cream

Ingredients:

For the praline:

- 1 cup granulated sugar
- 1/2 cup chopped nuts (such as almonds, pecans, or hazelnuts)

For the ice cream base:

- 2 cups heavy cream
- 1 cup whole milk
- 3/4 cup granulated sugar
- Pinch of salt
- 4 large egg yolks
- 1 teaspoon vanilla extract

Instructions:

To make the praline:

1. Line a baking sheet with parchment paper or a silicone baking mat.
2. In a heavy-bottomed saucepan, heat the granulated sugar over medium heat, stirring constantly with a heat-resistant spatula or wooden spoon. The sugar will clump and then melt into a golden amber liquid.
3. Once the sugar has melted and reached a deep amber color, quickly stir in the chopped nuts until evenly coated.
4. Immediately pour the hot praline mixture onto the prepared baking sheet, spreading it out thinly with a spatula. Let it cool completely, then break into small pieces or chop into chunks. Set aside.

To make the ice cream base:

1. In a saucepan, combine the heavy cream, whole milk, half of the sugar, and pinch of salt. Heat over medium heat, stirring occasionally, until the mixture is hot and just begins to bubble around the edges. Do not let it boil.
2. In a separate bowl, whisk the egg yolks with the remaining sugar until pale and slightly thickened.
3. Gradually pour about half of the hot cream mixture into the egg yolks, whisking constantly, to temper the yolks.

4. Pour the tempered egg mixture back into the saucepan with the remaining cream mixture. Cook over medium-low heat, stirring constantly, until the custard thickens slightly and coats the back of a spoon (about 170-175°F or 77-80°C). Do not let it boil.
5. Remove the saucepan from heat and stir in the vanilla extract.
6. Strain the custard through a fine-mesh sieve into a clean bowl to remove any bits of cooked egg.
7. Cover the bowl with plastic wrap, pressing it directly onto the surface of the custard to prevent a skin from forming. Chill in the refrigerator for at least 4 hours or overnight.

To assemble the Praline Ice Cream:

1. Once the custard base is chilled, churn it in an ice cream maker according to the manufacturer's instructions until it reaches a soft-serve consistency.
2. During the last few minutes of churning, add the chopped praline pieces into the ice cream maker, allowing them to mix evenly throughout the ice cream.
3. Transfer the churned ice cream with praline pieces to a freezer-safe container. Press a piece of parchment paper or plastic wrap directly onto the surface of the ice cream to prevent ice crystals from forming.
4. Freeze the ice cream for at least 4 hours or until firm.
5. Serve the Praline Ice Cream scooped into bowls or cones, garnished with additional praline pieces if desired.

Enjoy the creamy texture and sweet crunch of homemade Praline Ice Cream! This recipe makes about 1 quart of ice cream. Adjust the type of nuts used in the praline according to your preference.

Marsala Wine Gelato

Ingredients:

- 1 cup Marsala wine (sweet or dry, depending on your preference)
- 2 cups whole milk
- 1 cup heavy cream
- 3/4 cup granulated sugar
- Pinch of salt
- 4 large egg yolks
- 1 teaspoon vanilla extract

Instructions:

1. In a saucepan, combine the Marsala wine, whole milk, heavy cream, half of the sugar, and pinch of salt. Heat over medium heat, stirring occasionally, until the mixture is hot and just begins to bubble around the edges. Do not let it boil.
2. In a separate bowl, whisk the egg yolks with the remaining sugar until pale and slightly thickened.
3. Gradually pour about half of the hot Marsala cream mixture into the egg yolks, whisking constantly, to temper the yolks.
4. Pour the tempered egg mixture back into the saucepan with the remaining Marsala cream mixture. Cook over medium-low heat, stirring constantly, until the custard thickens slightly and coats the back of a spoon (about 170-175°F or 77-80°C). Do not let it boil.
5. Remove the saucepan from heat and stir in the vanilla extract.
6. Strain the custard through a fine-mesh sieve into a clean bowl to remove any bits of cooked egg.
7. Cover the bowl with plastic wrap, pressing it directly onto the surface of the custard to prevent a skin from forming. Chill in the refrigerator for at least 4 hours or overnight.
8. Once chilled, churn the Marsala custard in an ice cream maker according to the manufacturer's instructions until it reaches a soft-serve consistency.
9. Transfer the churned gelato to a freezer-safe container, press a piece of parchment paper or plastic wrap directly onto the surface, and freeze until firm (usually 4-6 hours).
10. Serve the Marsala Wine Gelato scooped into bowls or cones.

Enjoy the rich and nuanced flavors of homemade Marsala Wine Gelato! This recipe yields about 1 quart of gelato. Adjust the sweetness and intensity of Marsala wine flavor according to your taste preferences.

Watermelon Sorbet

Ingredients:

- 4 cups cubed seedless watermelon (about 1 small watermelon)
- 1/2 cup granulated sugar
- 1/4 cup water
- Juice of 1 lemon or lime

Instructions:

1. In a small saucepan, combine the granulated sugar and water. Heat over medium heat, stirring occasionally, until the sugar is completely dissolved. Remove from heat and let the syrup cool to room temperature.
2. In a blender or food processor, puree the cubed watermelon until smooth.
3. Pour the watermelon puree through a fine-mesh sieve into a bowl to remove any pulp or seeds.
4. Stir in the cooled sugar syrup and lemon or lime juice into the watermelon puree until well combined.
5. Cover the bowl with plastic wrap, pressing it directly onto the surface of the mixture to prevent a skin from forming. Chill the mixture in the refrigerator for at least 2 hours, or until thoroughly chilled.
6. Once chilled, pour the watermelon mixture into an ice cream maker and churn according to the manufacturer's instructions until it reaches a smooth and frozen consistency.
7. Transfer the sorbet to a freezer-safe container, cover with plastic wrap or a lid, and freeze for at least 4 hours or until firm.
8. Serve the Watermelon Sorbet scooped into bowls or cones, garnished with a slice of watermelon or mint leaves if desired.

Enjoy the cool and refreshing flavors of homemade Watermelon Sorbet! This recipe makes about 1 quart of sorbet. Adjust sweetness by varying the amount of sugar used, depending on the sweetness of the watermelon and your preference.

Earl Grey Lavender Ice Cream

Ingredients:

- 2 cups heavy cream
- 1 cup whole milk
- 3/4 cup granulated sugar
- 3 tablespoons loose Earl Grey tea leaves (or 4-5 Earl Grey tea bags)
- 2 tablespoons dried culinary lavender buds (food-grade)
- Pinch of salt
- 4 large egg yolks
- 1 teaspoon vanilla extract

Instructions:

1. In a saucepan, combine the heavy cream, whole milk, half of the sugar, Earl Grey tea leaves, dried lavender buds, and pinch of salt. Heat over medium heat, stirring occasionally, until the mixture is hot and just begins to bubble around the edges. Do not let it boil.
2. Remove the saucepan from heat, cover, and let the Earl Grey tea and lavender steep in the cream mixture for about 15-20 minutes to infuse the flavors. Stir occasionally.
3. Strain the infused cream mixture through a fine-mesh sieve into a clean saucepan, pressing on the tea leaves and lavender buds to extract all the liquid. Discard the solids.
4. In a separate bowl, whisk the egg yolks with the remaining sugar until pale and slightly thickened.
5. Gradually pour about half of the hot infused cream mixture into the egg yolks, whisking constantly, to temper the yolks.
6. Pour the tempered egg mixture back into the saucepan with the remaining infused cream mixture. Cook over medium-low heat, stirring constantly, until the custard thickens slightly and coats the back of a spoon (about 170-175°F or 77-80°C). Do not let it boil.
7. Remove the saucepan from heat and stir in the vanilla extract.
8. Strain the custard through a fine-mesh sieve into a clean bowl to remove any bits of cooked egg or tea leaves.
9. Cover the bowl with plastic wrap, pressing it directly onto the surface of the custard to prevent a skin from forming. Chill in the refrigerator for at least 4 hours or overnight.

10. Once chilled, churn the Earl Grey Lavender custard in an ice cream maker according to the manufacturer's instructions until it reaches a soft-serve consistency.
11. Transfer the churned ice cream to a freezer-safe container, press a piece of parchment paper or plastic wrap directly onto the surface, and freeze until firm (usually 4-6 hours).
12. Serve the Earl Grey Lavender Ice Cream scooped into bowls or cones.

Enjoy the fragrant and floral flavors of homemade Earl Grey Lavender Ice Cream! This recipe yields about 1 quart of ice cream. Adjust the intensity of Earl Grey and lavender flavors based on your preference.

Nutella Gelato

Ingredients:

- 1 cup whole milk
- 2 cups heavy cream
- 3/4 cup granulated sugar
- Pinch of salt
- 4 large egg yolks
- 1 teaspoon vanilla extract
- 1 cup Nutella (or any hazelnut chocolate spread)

Instructions:

1. In a saucepan, combine the whole milk, heavy cream, half of the sugar, and pinch of salt. Heat over medium heat, stirring occasionally, until the mixture is hot and just begins to bubble around the edges. Do not let it boil.
2. In a separate bowl, whisk the egg yolks with the remaining sugar until pale and slightly thickened.
3. Gradually pour about half of the hot cream mixture into the egg yolks, whisking constantly, to temper the yolks.
4. Pour the tempered egg mixture back into the saucepan with the remaining cream mixture. Cook over medium-low heat, stirring constantly, until the custard thickens slightly and coats the back of a spoon (about 170-175°F or 77-80°C). Do not let it boil.
5. Remove the saucepan from heat and stir in the vanilla extract.
6. Add the Nutella to the custard mixture and whisk until the Nutella is fully incorporated and the mixture is smooth and creamy.
7. Strain the Nutella custard through a fine-mesh sieve into a clean bowl to remove any bits of cooked egg.
8. Cover the bowl with plastic wrap, pressing it directly onto the surface of the custard to prevent a skin from forming. Chill in the refrigerator for at least 4 hours or overnight.
9. Once chilled, churn the Nutella custard in an ice cream maker according to the manufacturer's instructions until it reaches a soft-serve consistency.
10. Transfer the churned Nutella Gelato to a freezer-safe container, press a piece of parchment paper or plastic wrap directly onto the surface, and freeze until firm (usually 4-6 hours).
11. Serve the Nutella Gelato scooped into bowls or cones.

Enjoy the indulgent and creamy flavors of homemade Nutella Gelato! This recipe makes about 1 quart of gelato. Adjust sweetness by varying the amount of sugar used, depending on the sweetness of your Nutella and your preference.

Pear Sorbet

Ingredients:

- 4 ripe pears, peeled, cored, and chopped
- 1 cup water
- 3/4 cup granulated sugar
- Juice of 1 lemon

Instructions:

1. In a small saucepan, combine the water and granulated sugar. Heat over medium heat, stirring occasionally, until the sugar is completely dissolved. Remove from heat and let the syrup cool to room temperature.
2. In a blender or food processor, puree the chopped pears until smooth.
3. Pour the pear puree through a fine-mesh sieve into a bowl to remove any pulp or fibers.
4. Stir in the cooled sugar syrup and lemon juice into the pear puree until well combined.
5. Cover the bowl with plastic wrap, pressing it directly onto the surface of the mixture to prevent a skin from forming. Chill the mixture in the refrigerator for at least 2 hours, or until thoroughly chilled.
6. Once chilled, pour the pear mixture into an ice cream maker and churn according to the manufacturer's instructions until it reaches a smooth and frozen consistency.
7. Transfer the sorbet to a freezer-safe container, cover with plastic wrap or a lid, and freeze for at least 4 hours or until firm.
8. Serve the Pear Sorbet scooped into bowls or cones, garnished with a slice of pear or mint leaves if desired.

Enjoy the naturally sweet and refreshing flavors of homemade Pear Sorbet! This recipe makes about 1 quart of sorbet. Adjust sweetness by varying the amount of sugar used, depending on the ripeness and sweetness of the pears.

Salted Pistachio Ice Cream

Ingredients:

- 1 cup shelled pistachios
- 2 cups heavy cream
- 1 cup whole milk
- 3/4 cup granulated sugar
- Pinch of salt
- 4 large egg yolks
- 1 teaspoon vanilla extract

Instructions:

1. **Prepare the pistachios:**
     - Preheat your oven to 350°F (175°C).
     - Spread the pistachios evenly on a baking sheet.
     - Roast the pistachios in the oven for about 8-10 minutes, or until lightly golden and fragrant.
     - Remove from the oven and let them cool. Once cooled, roughly chop the pistachios. Set aside.
2. **Make the ice cream base:**
     - In a saucepan, combine the heavy cream, whole milk, half of the sugar, and pinch of salt. Heat over medium heat, stirring occasionally, until the mixture is hot and just begins to bubble around the edges. Do not let it boil.
3. **Infuse the pistachio flavor:**
     - Add the chopped pistachios to the hot cream mixture. Stir well and remove from heat.
     - Cover the saucepan and let the mixture steep for about 1 hour to infuse the pistachio flavor.
4. **Strain the pistachio-infused cream:**
     - After steeping, strain the mixture through a fine-mesh sieve into a clean bowl, pressing on the pistachios to extract all the liquid. Discard the solids.
5. **Prepare the custard:**
     - In a separate bowl, whisk the egg yolks with the remaining sugar until pale and slightly thickened.
     - Gradually pour about half of the hot pistachio-infused cream mixture into the egg yolks, whisking constantly, to temper the yolks.

- Pour the tempered egg mixture back into the saucepan with the remaining pistachio-infused cream. Cook over medium-low heat, stirring constantly, until the custard thickens slightly and coats the back of a spoon (about 170-175°F or 77-80°C). Do not let it boil.
- Remove from heat and stir in the vanilla extract.

6. **Chill the custard:**
   - Strain the custard through a fine-mesh sieve into a clean bowl to remove any bits of cooked egg.
   - Cover the bowl with plastic wrap, pressing it directly onto the surface of the custard to prevent a skin from forming. Chill in the refrigerator for at least 4 hours or overnight.

7. **Churn and freeze:**
   - Once chilled, churn the pistachio custard in an ice cream maker according to the manufacturer's instructions until it reaches a soft-serve consistency.
   - Transfer the churned ice cream to a freezer-safe container, press a piece of parchment paper or plastic wrap directly onto the surface, and freeze until firm (usually 4-6 hours).

8. **Serve:**
   - Serve the Salted Pistachio Ice Cream scooped into bowls or cones, garnished with additional chopped pistachios if desired.

Enjoy the creamy and nutty flavors of homemade Salted Pistachio Ice Cream! This recipe yields about 1 quart of ice cream. Adjust the level of saltiness by adding more or less salt according to your taste preference.

Lemon Thyme Gelato

Ingredients:

- 2 cups heavy cream
- 1 cup whole milk
- 3/4 cup granulated sugar
- Zest of 2 lemons
- 4-5 sprigs of fresh thyme (or 1 tablespoon dried thyme)
- Pinch of salt
- 4 large egg yolks
- Juice of 2 lemons
- 1 teaspoon vanilla extract

Instructions:

1. In a saucepan, combine the heavy cream, whole milk, half of the sugar, lemon zest, thyme sprigs (or dried thyme), and pinch of salt. Heat over medium heat, stirring occasionally, until the mixture is hot and just begins to bubble around the edges. Do not let it boil.
2. Remove the saucepan from heat, cover, and let the lemon zest and thyme steep in the cream mixture for about 15-20 minutes to infuse the flavors. Stir occasionally.
3. Strain the infused cream mixture through a fine-mesh sieve into a clean saucepan, pressing on the lemon zest and thyme to extract all the liquid. Discard the solids.
4. In a separate bowl, whisk the egg yolks with the remaining sugar until pale and slightly thickened.
5. Gradually pour about half of the hot infused cream mixture into the egg yolks, whisking constantly, to temper the yolks.
6. Pour the tempered egg mixture back into the saucepan with the remaining infused cream mixture. Cook over medium-low heat, stirring constantly, until the custard thickens slightly and coats the back of a spoon (about 170-175°F or 77-80°C). Do not let it boil.
7. Remove the saucepan from heat and stir in the lemon juice and vanilla extract.
8. Strain the custard through a fine-mesh sieve into a clean bowl to remove any bits of cooked egg or herbs.
9. Cover the bowl with plastic wrap, pressing it directly onto the surface of the custard to prevent a skin from forming. Chill in the refrigerator for at least 4 hours or overnight.

10. Once chilled, churn the Lemon Thyme custard in an ice cream maker according to the manufacturer's instructions until it reaches a soft-serve consistency.
11. Transfer the churned gelato to a freezer-safe container, press a piece of parchment paper or plastic wrap directly onto the surface, and freeze until firm (usually 4-6 hours).
12. Serve the Lemon Thyme Gelato scooped into bowls or cones.

Enjoy the refreshing and aromatic flavors of homemade Lemon Thyme Gelato! This recipe makes about 1 quart of gelato. Adjust the intensity of lemon and thyme flavors based on your preference.

Plum Sorbet

Ingredients:

- 4 cups ripe plums, pitted and chopped (about 6-8 plums)
- 1 cup water
- 3/4 cup granulated sugar
- Juice of 1 lemon

Instructions:

1. In a small saucepan, combine the water and granulated sugar. Heat over medium heat, stirring occasionally, until the sugar is completely dissolved. Remove from heat and let the syrup cool to room temperature.
2. In a blender or food processor, puree the chopped plums until smooth.
3. Pour the plum puree through a fine-mesh sieve into a bowl to remove any skins or fibers.
4. Stir in the cooled sugar syrup and lemon juice into the plum puree until well combined.
5. Cover the bowl with plastic wrap, pressing it directly onto the surface of the mixture to prevent a skin from forming. Chill the mixture in the refrigerator for at least 2 hours, or until thoroughly chilled.
6. Once chilled, pour the plum mixture into an ice cream maker and churn according to the manufacturer's instructions until it reaches a smooth and frozen consistency.
7. Transfer the sorbet to a freezer-safe container, cover with plastic wrap or a lid, and freeze for at least 4 hours or until firm.
8. Serve the Plum Sorbet scooped into bowls or cones, garnished with a slice of plum or mint leaves if desired.

Enjoy the refreshing and fruity flavors of homemade Plum Sorbet! This recipe makes about 1 quart of sorbet. Adjust sweetness by varying the amount of sugar used, depending on the sweetness of the plums and your preference.

Spiced Apple Ice Cream

Ingredients:

- 2 cups heavy cream
- 1 cup whole milk
- 3/4 cup granulated sugar
- 4 large egg yolks
- 1 teaspoon vanilla extract
- 2 cups applesauce (unsweetened)
- 1 teaspoon ground cinnamon
- 1/2 teaspoon ground nutmeg
- 1/4 teaspoon ground cloves
- Pinch of salt

Instructions:

1. In a saucepan, combine the heavy cream, whole milk, half of the sugar, ground cinnamon, ground nutmeg, ground cloves, and pinch of salt. Heat over medium heat, stirring occasionally, until the mixture is hot and just begins to bubble around the edges. Do not let it boil.
2. In a separate bowl, whisk the egg yolks with the remaining sugar until pale and slightly thickened.
3. Gradually pour about half of the hot spiced cream mixture into the egg yolks, whisking constantly, to temper the yolks.
4. Pour the tempered egg mixture back into the saucepan with the remaining spiced cream mixture. Cook over medium-low heat, stirring constantly, until the custard thickens slightly and coats the back of a spoon (about 170-175°F or 77-80°C). Do not let it boil.
5. Remove the saucepan from heat and stir in the vanilla extract.
6. Stir in the applesauce until well combined with the custard mixture.
7. Strain the custard through a fine-mesh sieve into a clean bowl to remove any bits of cooked egg or spices.
8. Cover the bowl with plastic wrap, pressing it directly onto the surface of the custard to prevent a skin from forming. Chill in the refrigerator for at least 4 hours or overnight.
9. Once chilled, churn the spiced apple custard in an ice cream maker according to the manufacturer's instructions until it reaches a soft-serve consistency.

10. Transfer the churned ice cream to a freezer-safe container, press a piece of parchment paper or plastic wrap directly onto the surface, and freeze until firm (usually 4-6 hours).
11. Serve the Spiced Apple Ice Cream scooped into bowls or cones, garnished with a sprinkle of cinnamon if desired.

Enjoy the warm and cozy flavors of homemade Spiced Apple Ice Cream! This recipe makes about 1 quart of ice cream. Adjust the spices and sweetness according to your taste preference and the tartness of your applesauce.

Chocolate Hazelnut Gelato

Ingredients:

- 1 cup hazelnuts, toasted and skins removed
- 2 cups whole milk
- 1 cup heavy cream
- 3/4 cup granulated sugar
- Pinch of salt
- 4 large egg yolks
- 1 teaspoon vanilla extract
- 6 ounces semisweet or dark chocolate, finely chopped

Instructions:

1. **Prepare the hazelnuts:**
     - Preheat your oven to 350°F (175°C).
     - Spread the hazelnuts evenly on a baking sheet.
     - Roast the hazelnuts in the oven for about 10-12 minutes, or until lightly golden and fragrant.
     - Remove from the oven and let them cool slightly. Rub them in a kitchen towel to remove the skins.
     - Chop the hazelnuts finely. Set aside.
2. **Make the gelato base:**
     - In a saucepan, combine the whole milk, heavy cream, half of the sugar, and pinch of salt. Heat over medium heat, stirring occasionally, until the mixture is hot and just begins to bubble around the edges. Do not let it boil.
3. **Prepare the chocolate mixture:**
     - Place the finely chopped chocolate in a heatproof bowl.
     - In a separate bowl, whisk the egg yolks with the remaining sugar until pale and slightly thickened.
4. **Temper the eggs:**
     - Gradually pour about half of the hot milk mixture into the egg yolks, whisking constantly, to temper the yolks.
     - Pour the tempered egg mixture back into the saucepan with the remaining milk mixture. Cook over medium-low heat, stirring constantly, until the custard thickens slightly and coats the back of a spoon (about 170-175°F or 77-80°C). Do not let it boil.
5. **Combine the gelato base with chocolate and hazelnuts:**

- Remove the saucepan from heat and immediately pour the hot custard over the chopped chocolate.
- Let it sit for a minute, then stir until the chocolate is completely melted and incorporated into the custard.
- Stir in the vanilla extract and chopped hazelnuts.

6. **Chill the gelato base:**
   - Strain the gelato base through a fine-mesh sieve into a clean bowl to remove any bits of cooked egg.
   - Cover the bowl with plastic wrap, pressing it directly onto the surface of the custard to prevent a skin from forming. Chill in the refrigerator for at least 4 hours or overnight.

7. **Churn and freeze:**
   - Once chilled, churn the Chocolate Hazelnut custard in an ice cream maker according to the manufacturer's instructions until it reaches a soft-serve consistency.

8. **Final freezing:**
   - Transfer the churned gelato to a freezer-safe container, press a piece of parchment paper or plastic wrap directly onto the surface, and freeze until firm (usually 4-6 hours).

9. **Serve:**
   - Serve the Chocolate Hazelnut Gelato scooped into bowls or cones, garnished with additional chopped hazelnuts or chocolate shavings if desired.

Enjoy the creamy, nutty, and chocolatey flavors of homemade Chocolate Hazelnut Gelato! This recipe makes about 1 quart of gelato. Adjust sweetness by varying the amount of sugar used, depending on the sweetness of your chocolate and your preference.

Fig Sorbet

Ingredients:

- 1 pound fresh figs (about 10-12 figs), stems removed and chopped
- 1 cup water
- 3/4 cup granulated sugar
- Juice of 1 lemon

Instructions:

1. In a small saucepan, combine the water and granulated sugar. Heat over medium heat, stirring occasionally, until the sugar is completely dissolved. Remove from heat and let the syrup cool to room temperature.
2. In a blender or food processor, puree the chopped figs until smooth.
3. Pour the fig puree through a fine-mesh sieve into a bowl to remove any seeds or chunks.
4. Stir in the cooled sugar syrup and lemon juice into the fig puree until well combined.
5. Cover the bowl with plastic wrap, pressing it directly onto the surface of the mixture to prevent a skin from forming. Chill the mixture in the refrigerator for at least 2 hours, or until thoroughly chilled.
6. Once chilled, pour the fig mixture into an ice cream maker and churn according to the manufacturer's instructions until it reaches a smooth and frozen consistency.
7. Transfer the sorbet to a freezer-safe container, cover with plastic wrap or a lid, and freeze for at least 4 hours or until firm.
8. Serve the Fig Sorbet scooped into bowls or cones, garnished with a slice of fresh fig or mint leaves if desired.

Enjoy the sweet and fruity flavors of homemade Fig Sorbet! This recipe makes about 1 quart of sorbet. Adjust sweetness by varying the amount of sugar used, depending on the ripeness and sweetness of the figs.

Honey Lavender Ice Cream

Ingredients:

- 2 cups heavy cream
- 1 cup whole milk
- 1/2 cup honey
- 1/4 cup dried culinary lavender buds (food-grade)
- Pinch of salt
- 4 large egg yolks
- 1 teaspoon vanilla extract

Instructions:

1. In a saucepan, combine the heavy cream, whole milk, honey, dried lavender buds, and pinch of salt. Heat over medium heat, stirring occasionally, until the mixture is hot and just begins to bubble around the edges. Do not let it boil.
2. Remove the saucepan from heat, cover, and let the lavender steep in the cream mixture for about 15-20 minutes to infuse the flavors. Stir occasionally.
3. Strain the infused cream mixture through a fine-mesh sieve into a clean saucepan, pressing on the lavender buds to extract all the liquid. Discard the solids.
4. In a separate bowl, whisk the egg yolks until smooth.
5. Gradually pour about half of the hot infused cream mixture into the egg yolks, whisking constantly, to temper the yolks.
6. Pour the tempered egg mixture back into the saucepan with the remaining infused cream mixture. Cook over medium-low heat, stirring constantly, until the custard thickens slightly and coats the back of a spoon (about 170-175°F or 77-80°C). Do not let it boil.
7. Remove the saucepan from heat and stir in the vanilla extract.
8. Strain the custard through a fine-mesh sieve into a clean bowl to remove any bits of cooked egg or lavender.
9. Cover the bowl with plastic wrap, pressing it directly onto the surface of the custard to prevent a skin from forming. Chill in the refrigerator for at least 4 hours or overnight.
10. Once chilled, churn the Honey Lavender custard in an ice cream maker according to the manufacturer's instructions until it reaches a soft-serve consistency.
11. Transfer the churned ice cream to a freezer-safe container, press a piece of parchment paper or plastic wrap directly onto the surface, and freeze until firm (usually 4-6 hours).

12. Serve the Honey Lavender Ice Cream scooped into bowls or cones, garnished with a sprinkle of dried lavender buds or a drizzle of honey if desired.

Enjoy the delicate and aromatic flavors of homemade Honey Lavender Ice Cream! This recipe makes about 1 quart of ice cream. Adjust sweetness by varying the amount of honey used, depending on your taste preference.

Coconut Lime Gelato

Ingredients:

- 1 can (13.5 oz) coconut milk (full-fat)
- 1 cup heavy cream
- 3/4 cup granulated sugar
- Zest of 2 limes
- 1/2 cup freshly squeezed lime juice (about 4-5 limes)
- Pinch of salt
- 4 large egg yolks
- 1 teaspoon vanilla extract

Instructions:

1. In a saucepan, combine the coconut milk, heavy cream, half of the sugar, lime zest, lime juice, and pinch of salt. Heat over medium heat, stirring occasionally, until the mixture is hot and just begins to bubble around the edges. Do not let it boil.
2. In a separate bowl, whisk the egg yolks with the remaining sugar until pale and slightly thickened.
3. Gradually pour about half of the hot coconut-lime mixture into the egg yolks, whisking constantly, to temper the yolks.
4. Pour the tempered egg mixture back into the saucepan with the remaining coconut-lime mixture. Cook over medium-low heat, stirring constantly, until the custard thickens slightly and coats the back of a spoon (about 170-175°F or 77-80°C). Do not let it boil.
5. Remove the saucepan from heat and stir in the vanilla extract.
6. Strain the custard through a fine-mesh sieve into a clean bowl to remove any bits of cooked egg or lime zest.
7. Cover the bowl with plastic wrap, pressing it directly onto the surface of the custard to prevent a skin from forming. Chill in the refrigerator for at least 4 hours or overnight.
8. Once chilled, churn the Coconut Lime custard in an ice cream maker according to the manufacturer's instructions until it reaches a soft-serve consistency.
9. Transfer the churned gelato to a freezer-safe container, press a piece of parchment paper or plastic wrap directly onto the surface, and freeze until firm (usually 4-6 hours).
10. Serve the Coconut Lime Gelato scooped into bowls or cones, garnished with a slice of lime or toasted coconut flakes if desired.

Enjoy the tropical and tangy flavors of homemade Coconut Lime Gelato! This recipe makes about 1 quart of gelato. Adjust sweetness by varying the amount of sugar used, depending on the tartness of your limes and your preference.

Mango Passion Fruit Sorbet

Ingredients:

- 2 ripe mangoes, peeled, pitted, and chopped (about 2 cups)
- Pulp of 4-5 ripe passion fruits (about 1/2 cup)
- 1 cup water
- 3/4 cup granulated sugar
- Juice of 1 lemon

Instructions:

1. In a small saucepan, combine the water and granulated sugar. Heat over medium heat, stirring occasionally, until the sugar is completely dissolved. Remove from heat and let the syrup cool to room temperature.
2. In a blender or food processor, puree the chopped mangoes until smooth.
3. Pour the mango puree through a fine-mesh sieve into a bowl to remove any fibers or chunks. Press with a spoon to extract as much liquid as possible.
4. Add the passion fruit pulp to the mango puree and stir well to combine.
5. Stir in the cooled sugar syrup and lemon juice into the mango-passion fruit mixture until well combined.
6. Cover the bowl with plastic wrap, pressing it directly onto the surface of the mixture to prevent a skin from forming. Chill the mixture in the refrigerator for at least 2 hours, or until thoroughly chilled.
7. Once chilled, pour the sorbet mixture into an ice cream maker and churn according to the manufacturer's instructions until it reaches a smooth and frozen consistency.
8. Transfer the sorbet to a freezer-safe container, cover with plastic wrap or a lid, and freeze for at least 4 hours or until firm.
9. Serve the Mango Passion Fruit Sorbet scooped into bowls or cones, garnished with a slice of mango or passion fruit if desired.

Enjoy the tropical and tangy flavors of homemade Mango Passion Fruit Sorbet! This recipe makes about 1 quart of sorbet. Adjust sweetness by varying the amount of sugar used, depending on the ripeness and sweetness of the mangoes and passion fruits.

Brown Butter Pecan Ice Cream

Ingredients:

- 1 cup pecan halves
- 6 tablespoons unsalted butter
- 1 cup whole milk
- 2 cups heavy cream
- 3/4 cup granulated sugar
- Pinch of salt
- 4 large egg yolks
- 1 teaspoon vanilla extract

Instructions:

1. **Toast the pecans:**
    - Preheat your oven to 350°F (175°C).
    - Spread the pecan halves evenly on a baking sheet.
    - Toast the pecans in the oven for about 8-10 minutes, or until fragrant and lightly toasted. Keep an eye on them to prevent burning. Remove from the oven and let them cool. Once cooled, roughly chop them. Set aside.
2. **Brown the butter:**
    - In a small saucepan, melt the butter over medium heat. Continue cooking, stirring frequently, until the butter solids turn golden brown and emit a nutty aroma, about 5-7 minutes. Watch carefully to prevent burning.
    - Once browned, immediately remove from heat and pour the browned butter into a heatproof bowl. Let it cool slightly.
3. **Prepare the ice cream base:**
    - In a saucepan, combine the whole milk, heavy cream, half of the sugar, and pinch of salt. Heat over medium heat, stirring occasionally, until the mixture is hot and just begins to bubble around the edges. Do not let it boil.
4. **Temper the eggs:**
    - In a separate bowl, whisk the egg yolks with the remaining sugar until pale and slightly thickened.
    - Gradually pour about half of the hot cream mixture into the egg yolks, whisking constantly, to temper the yolks.
5. **Combine the custard:**
    - Pour the tempered egg mixture back into the saucepan with the remaining cream mixture. Cook over medium-low heat, stirring constantly, until the

custard thickens slightly and coats the back of a spoon (about 170-175°F or 77-80°C). Do not let it boil.
6. **Incorporate the brown butter and pecans:**
    - Remove the saucepan from heat and slowly whisk in the browned butter until fully incorporated.
    - Stir in the vanilla extract.
    - Fold in the chopped toasted pecans.
7. **Chill the custard:**
    - Strain the custard through a fine-mesh sieve into a clean bowl to remove any bits of cooked egg or pecan pieces.
    - Cover the bowl with plastic wrap, pressing it directly onto the surface of the custard to prevent a skin from forming. Chill in the refrigerator for at least 4 hours or overnight.
8. **Churn and freeze:**
    - Once chilled, churn the Brown Butter Pecan custard in an ice cream maker according to the manufacturer's instructions until it reaches a soft-serve consistency.
9. **Final freezing:**
    - Transfer the churned ice cream to a freezer-safe container, press a piece of parchment paper or plastic wrap directly onto the surface, and freeze until firm (usually 4-6 hours).
10. **Serve:**
    - Serve the Brown Butter Pecan Ice Cream scooped into bowls or cones, garnished with additional toasted pecans if desired.

Enjoy the rich, nutty, and buttery flavors of homemade Brown Butter Pecan Ice Cream! This recipe makes about 1 quart of ice cream. Adjust sweetness and nuttiness according to your taste preference.

Rosewater Pistachio Gelato

Ingredients:

- 1 cup shelled pistachios, unsalted
- 2 cups whole milk
- 1 cup heavy cream
- 3/4 cup granulated sugar
- Pinch of salt
- 4 large egg yolks
- 1 teaspoon vanilla extract
- 1-2 tablespoons rosewater (adjust to taste)
- 1/4 cup chopped pistachios, toasted (optional, for garnish)

Instructions:

1. **Toast and process the pistachios:**
    - Preheat your oven to 350°F (175°C).
    - Spread the pistachios evenly on a baking sheet.
    - Toast the pistachios in the oven for about 8-10 minutes, or until lightly golden and fragrant. Keep an eye on them to prevent burning.
    - Remove from the oven and let them cool completely. Once cooled, finely chop or process them in a food processor until they are finely ground but still have some texture. Set aside.
2. **Prepare the gelato base:**
    - In a saucepan, combine the whole milk, heavy cream, half of the sugar, and pinch of salt. Heat over medium heat, stirring occasionally, until the mixture is hot and just begins to bubble around the edges. Do not let it boil.
3. **Temper the eggs:**
    - In a separate bowl, whisk the egg yolks with the remaining sugar until pale and slightly thickened.
    - Gradually pour about half of the hot cream mixture into the egg yolks, whisking constantly, to temper the yolks.
4. **Cook the custard:**
    - Pour the tempered egg mixture back into the saucepan with the remaining cream mixture. Cook over medium-low heat, stirring constantly, until the custard thickens slightly and coats the back of a spoon (about 170-175°F or 77-80°C). Do not let it boil.
5. **Incorporate the flavors:**

- Remove the saucepan from heat and stir in the vanilla extract and rosewater. Start with 1 tablespoon of rosewater, taste, and add more if desired for stronger flavor.
- Stir in the finely ground pistachios until well combined.

6. **Chill the custard:**
    - Strain the custard through a fine-mesh sieve into a clean bowl to remove any bits of cooked egg or pistachio pieces.
    - Cover the bowl with plastic wrap, pressing it directly onto the surface of the custard to prevent a skin from forming. Chill in the refrigerator for at least 4 hours or overnight.

7. **Churn and freeze:**
    - Once chilled, churn the Rosewater Pistachio custard in an ice cream maker according to the manufacturer's instructions until it reaches a soft-serve consistency.

8. **Final freezing:**
    - Transfer the churned gelato to a freezer-safe container, press a piece of parchment paper or plastic wrap directly onto the surface, and sprinkle with chopped toasted pistachios if desired.
    - Freeze until firm (usually 4-6 hours).

9. **Serve:**
    - Serve the Rosewater Pistachio Gelato scooped into bowls or cones, garnished with additional chopped toasted pistachios if desired.

Enjoy the exotic and luxurious flavors of homemade Rosewater Pistachio Gelato! This recipe makes about 1 quart of gelato. Adjust sweetness and rosewater intensity according to your preference for a delightful dessert experience.

Apricot Sorbet

Ingredients:

- 1 pound fresh apricots (about 8-10 apricots), pitted and chopped
- 1 cup water
- 3/4 cup granulated sugar
- Juice of 1 lemon

Instructions:

1. In a small saucepan, combine the water and granulated sugar. Heat over medium heat, stirring occasionally, until the sugar is completely dissolved. Remove from heat and let the syrup cool to room temperature.
2. In a blender or food processor, puree the chopped apricots until smooth.
3. Pour the apricot puree through a fine-mesh sieve into a bowl to remove any skins or fibers.
4. Stir in the cooled sugar syrup and lemon juice into the apricot puree until well combined.
5. Cover the bowl with plastic wrap, pressing it directly onto the surface of the mixture to prevent a skin from forming. Chill the mixture in the refrigerator for at least 2 hours, or until thoroughly chilled.
6. Once chilled, pour the apricot mixture into an ice cream maker and churn according to the manufacturer's instructions until it reaches a smooth and frozen consistency.
7. Transfer the sorbet to a freezer-safe container, cover with plastic wrap or a lid, and freeze for at least 4 hours or until firm.
8. Serve the Apricot Sorbet scooped into bowls or cones, garnished with a slice of apricot or mint leaves if desired.

Enjoy the bright and fruity flavors of homemade Apricot Sorbet! This recipe makes about 1 quart of sorbet. Adjust sweetness by varying the amount of sugar used, depending on the ripeness and sweetness of the apricots.

Bourbon Vanilla Ice Cream

Ingredients:

- 2 cups heavy cream
- 1 cup whole milk
- 3/4 cup granulated sugar
- Pinch of salt
- 4 large egg yolks
- 1 teaspoon vanilla extract
- 2 tablespoons bourbon whiskey

Instructions:

1. In a saucepan, combine the heavy cream, whole milk, half of the sugar, and pinch of salt. Heat over medium heat, stirring occasionally, until the mixture is hot and just begins to bubble around the edges. Do not let it boil.
2. In a separate bowl, whisk the egg yolks with the remaining sugar until pale and slightly thickened.
3. Gradually pour about half of the hot cream mixture into the egg yolks, whisking constantly, to temper the yolks.
4. Pour the tempered egg mixture back into the saucepan with the remaining cream mixture. Cook over medium-low heat, stirring constantly, until the custard thickens slightly and coats the back of a spoon (about 170-175°F or 77-80°C). Do not let it boil.
5. Remove the saucepan from heat and stir in the vanilla extract and bourbon whiskey.
6. Strain the custard through a fine-mesh sieve into a clean bowl to remove any bits of cooked egg.
7. Cover the bowl with plastic wrap, pressing it directly onto the surface of the custard to prevent a skin from forming. Chill in the refrigerator for at least 4 hours or overnight.
8. Once chilled, churn the Bourbon Vanilla custard in an ice cream maker according to the manufacturer's instructions until it reaches a soft-serve consistency.
9. Transfer the churned ice cream to a freezer-safe container, press a piece of parchment paper or plastic wrap directly onto the surface, and freeze until firm (usually 4-6 hours).
10. Serve the Bourbon Vanilla Ice Cream scooped into bowls or cones, garnished with a drizzle of bourbon or shaved chocolate if desired.

Enjoy the creamy and subtly boozy flavors of homemade Bourbon Vanilla Ice Cream! This recipe makes about 1 quart of ice cream. Adjust the amount of bourbon according to your taste preference.

Dark Chocolate Gelato

Ingredients:

- 2 cups whole milk
- 1 cup heavy cream
- 3/4 cup granulated sugar
- Pinch of salt
- 4 ounces dark chocolate (at least 70% cocoa), finely chopped
- 4 large egg yolks
- 1 teaspoon vanilla extract

Instructions:

1. In a saucepan, combine the whole milk, heavy cream, half of the sugar, and pinch of salt. Heat over medium heat, stirring occasionally, until the mixture is hot and just begins to bubble around the edges. Do not let it boil.
2. Place the finely chopped dark chocolate in a heatproof bowl.
3. In a separate bowl, whisk the egg yolks with the remaining sugar until pale and slightly thickened.
4. Gradually pour about half of the hot milk mixture into the egg yolks, whisking constantly, to temper the yolks.
5. Pour the tempered egg mixture back into the saucepan with the remaining milk mixture. Cook over medium-low heat, stirring constantly, until the custard thickens slightly and coats the back of a spoon (about 170-175°F or 77-80°C). Do not let it boil.
6. Immediately pour the hot custard over the chopped dark chocolate. Let it sit for a minute to melt the chocolate, then stir until smooth and well combined.
7. Stir in the vanilla extract.
8. Strain the chocolate custard through a fine-mesh sieve into a clean bowl to remove any bits of cooked egg or chocolate pieces.
9. Cover the bowl with plastic wrap, pressing it directly onto the surface of the custard to prevent a skin from forming. Chill in the refrigerator for at least 4 hours or overnight.
10. Once chilled, churn the Dark Chocolate custard in an ice cream maker according to the manufacturer's instructions until it reaches a soft-serve consistency.
11. Transfer the churned gelato to a freezer-safe container, press a piece of parchment paper or plastic wrap directly onto the surface, and freeze until firm (usually 4-6 hours).

12. Serve the Dark Chocolate Gelato scooped into bowls or cones, garnished with chocolate shavings or cocoa powder if desired.

Enjoy the rich, deep chocolate flavor of homemade Dark Chocolate Gelato! This recipe makes about 1 quart of gelato. Adjust sweetness by varying the amount of sugar used, depending on the bitterness of your dark chocolate and your preference.

Champagne Sorbet

Ingredients:

- 1 cup water
- 1 cup granulated sugar
- 1 bottle (750 ml) champagne or sparkling wine (choose a dry variety)
- Juice of 1 lemon
- Zest of 1 lemon (optional, for added flavor)

Instructions:

1. In a small saucepan, combine the water and granulated sugar. Heat over medium heat, stirring occasionally, until the sugar is completely dissolved. Remove from heat and let the syrup cool to room temperature.
2. Once the sugar syrup is cooled, pour it into a large bowl.
3. Stir in the champagne or sparkling wine, lemon juice, and lemon zest (if using) into the sugar syrup until well combined.
4. Cover the bowl with plastic wrap and chill the mixture in the refrigerator for at least 2 hours, or until thoroughly chilled.
5. Once chilled, pour the champagne mixture into an ice cream maker and churn according to the manufacturer's instructions until it reaches a soft-serve consistency.
6. Transfer the sorbet to a freezer-safe container, cover with plastic wrap or a lid, and freeze for at least 4 hours or until firm.
7. Serve the Champagne Sorbet scooped into chilled bowls or champagne flutes for an extra touch of elegance.

Enjoy the refreshing and bubbly flavors of homemade Champagne Sorbet! This recipe makes about 1 quart of sorbet. Adjust sweetness by varying the amount of sugar used, depending on your preference and the sweetness of the champagne or sparkling wine used.